Spooky Magic Tricks

David Knoles

 Sterling Publishing Co., Inc. New York

For Dorothy Ciffone
who believed in the magic

Library of Congress Cataloging-in-Publication Data

Knoles, David.
 Spooky magic tricks / David Knoles.
  p. cm.
 Includes index.
 ISBN 0-8069-0418-6
 1. Conjuring—Juvenile literature. 2. Tricks—Juvenile
literature. I. Title.
GV1548.K58 1993
793.8—dc20   93-1642
                                                  CIP
                                                  AC

10 9 8 7 6 5 4 3 2

First paperback edition published in 1994 by
Sterling Publishing Company, Inc.
387 Park Avenue South, New York, N.Y. 10016
© 1993 by David Knoles
Distributed in Canada by Sterling Publishing
% Canadian Manda Group, P.O. Box 920, Station U
Toronto, Ontario, Canada M8Z 5P9
Distributed in Great Britain and Europe by Cassell PLC
Villiers House, 41/47 Strand, London WC2N 5JE, England
Distributed in Australia by Capricorn Link (Australia) Pty Ltd.
P.O. Box 6651, Baulkham Hills, Business Centre, NSW 2153, Australia
Manufactured in the United States of America
All rights reserved

Cover design by Jim Sharpe

Sterling ISBN 0-8069-0418-6 Trade
              0-8069-0419-4 Paper

Contents

Before the Spell Is Cast

There's a spell on this house.

An evil wind whistles through the broken windows. Leathery bat wings rustle in the attic. Mournful voices echo through the halls.

The house is haunted and the air is alive with mystery and scary magic.

But the ghosts aren't harmful. These ghouls just want to have fun. And you will use spooky magic to bring their restless spirits to life.

But before you enter this creepy crypt, there are a few things you need to know.

Probably the first trick anyone bought from the display wall of a magic shop lured them with the claim "No Skill Required!"

If you believed that claim, you probably found out you were fooling yourself.

Magic is a skill. Even the simplest, self-working trick takes skill to perform. And the only way to get this kind of magical skill is by practice.

The word "practice" might sound about as much fun as the word "homework," but it really isn't as bad as it seems. Practicing magic is not ony fun, but it's rewarding as well.

The ghostly effects in *Spooky Magic Tricks*, for example, were chosen for their simplicity. But even though they are easy to learn and perform, they still take practice.

Practice each trick as often as possible. In fact, you can't practice often enough. Practice each move over and over until you can do it without thinking.

You may have also heard the phrase "Magic is all done with mirrors." In a sense, this is true because the best way to practice magic tricks is in front of a mirror. When you practice in a mirror, you see tricks just as the audience will see them. That makes it a lot easier to learn to perform the moves smoothly, stand in the right position and hold the props at the proper angles so that you don't accidentally expose the secrets of the tricks.

Practicing in front of a mirror will also give you a sense of timing. Pacing is as important to a magician as it is to a comedian. A successful, well-executed, well-timed trick is like a story. It has a beginning, a middle and an end. You have to pace each trick so there is a buildup of mystery. If you rush through it, the mystery will be lost. If, on the other hand, you drag a trick out too long, spectators could lose interest.

Remember that magic is a pure product of the imagination. Aided by the subtle manipulation of ordinary objects in sly and secret ways, it presents the unexpected appearance of supernatural powers and creates a sense of wonder.

But the wonder—the magic—doesn't lie in the secret workings of the tricks alone. It's born in your mind. In a sense, you become a guide who will lead spectators to the conclusion that what they see is *truly* magical.

This isn't as hard as it sounds. All you really need to do to accomplish this seeming miracle is use your imagination and pretend.

It's just like acting. All actors are really just pretending. That's what acting is about. They are assuming the role of a fictitious character in much the same way a kid playing in the yard pretends he's Batman or James Bond.

Being a magician isn't any different. A magician may be using props, misdirection and sleight-of-hand, but he's still playing out a role. A magician knows his effects are just clever tricks and not the breaking of natural laws. And yet, his effects will truly appear magical if he uses his acting ability to pretend to react to both the audience and the manipulation of the tricks as if they *are* violations of natural laws and he *has* special powers.

Once you get a feel for the look and timing of each illusion, you will begin to tailor your performance to suit your own style. You can make it serious and spooky or make it silly and play it for laughs. But above all, make it fun. You are out to entertain and surprise your audience, not to make the people feel foolish or ridiculous. And if someone does occasionally figure out the workings of a trick, don't worry about it. It's not the end of the world. Laugh it off and move on.

Later, go back and practice the trick until it's perfect.

If you follow these tips and the instructions that follow, you will find yourself not only becoming an absolute wizard in a lot less time than you might have imagined, but having a lot of fun doing it.

Now that you know what magic is all about, it's time to begin. The old door is creaking inward, and the ghosts are growing restless. Step inside and weave your spooky spell . . .

1. Did Somebody See a Ghost?

Ask people if they've ever seen a ghost and see what happens.

Whether it's the story of an actual ghostly encounter, a tale of objects being thrown around a room or just a creepy feeling in an empty hallway, everyone has a story to tell.

Some people take ghosts seriously while others take the whole subject with a giant grain of salt.

But whichever is the case, here are some fun phantom feats you can use to convince your audience it's seen the real thing!

A Spooky Knot

Take out a pocket handkerchief and let it hang from the fingertips of your right hand.

Say: "You can always tell when there's a ghost around. They like to play pranks. They like to tie knots in things without you knowing about it. I'll show you what I mean."

Lift the corner of the handkerchief with your left hand and hold it with your right fingertips. Shake it out with a snap. No knot appears.

Say: "I guess there's no ghost around here."

Try it again. Still no knot.

Say: "Maybe he's just shy. Maybe if we ask him nicely, he'll come out."

Shake the handkerchief loose one more time.

This time, to everyone's surprise, there is suddenly a knot tied in the end of the handkerchief.

This is an easy, but very effective illusion. Begin by tying a knot in the corner of a handkerchief. Hold the end with the knot in your right hand so it is hidden by your fingers (1).

Gather the other end of the handkerchief in your hand (2).

The first two times you shake out the handkerchief, release the end without the knot.

The last time you shake it out, release the end with the knot (3).

It will look to your audience as if a knot appeared in the handkerchief from nowhere.

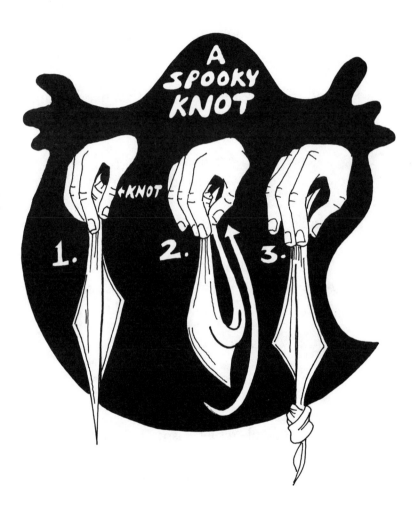

The Spirited Handkerchief

Show a handkerchief with a knot tied on one of its ends and then drape it over the palm of your right hand.

Say: "Ghosts tie knots in things because they like to hide in there and use that object—like the bodies they no longer have."

Suddenly, the knotted end of the handkerchief stands straight up, quivers for a moment, then falls back down.

Say: "There's a ghost in here all right. We have to be careful. Once they show themselves, sometimes they try to get away."

The handkerchief stands upright abruptly, then seems to try to fly out of your hand. You have to catch it with your left hand to keep it from getting away.

Say: "He was trying to fly away. He must be in high spirits."

"The Spirited Handkerchief" isn't as ordinary as it appears. In order to make it work, push a short piece of wire under the hem of the handkerchief against the knot.

To make it rise and fall, push against the edge of the hidden wire with your thumb.

To make it try to fly away, simply extend your hand

as if the handkerchief were flying away and you were just hanging on to it. Reach out and grab the knot with your other hand.

Drape it over the other hand to make it rise again.

WIRE IN HEM

The Phantom Tube

A plain, white pocket handkerchief rests on a table beside a metal tube (a tin can) sealed on both ends with plastic lids. Pick up the handkerchief and wad it into a ball.

Say: "Ghosts like to hide in handkerchiefs so you won't know what they really look like."

Pick up the tube and remove the lid on top. Show that it's empty. Put the handkerchief inside and re-place the lid. Set the can back on the table.

Say: "Sometimes, if they like you, the ghosts will show themselves as they *really* are."

Pick up the tube and remove the lid again. Reach inside.

Instead of a white handkerchief, there's a white ghost in there with a round head and two, empty black eyes!

The secret is in the tube, which has a false bottom in the middle painted black, and two identical lids on the ends.

The small ghost (described in the next trick, "The Floating Ghost") is inside the lower section of the tube before the trick begins.

When you open the upper part, it appears to be an ordinary, metal tube. Holding the tube on the palm of your left hand, you place the handkerchief inside the upper compartment. Turn your left hand over as in illustration 2, turning the tube over as well, and place it on the table. Now the compartment containing the ghost is on top.

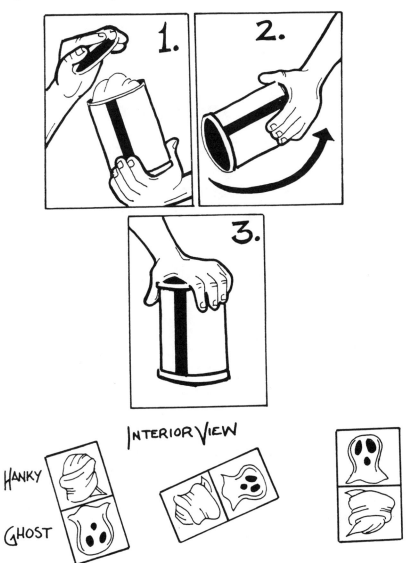

INTERIOR VIEW

HANKY

GHOST

Pick up the tube again, remove the lid and pull out the ghost. Turn the tube toward the audience and show it is now empty.

People will think they've seen a hanky become a ghost before their very eyes.

(Instructions for making "The Phantom Tube" appear in Chapter 7, "Spooky Props.")

The Floating Ghost

Hold a small, round-headed "ghost" with black eyes and moaning mouth directly in front of you between the fingers of both hands.

Say: "This little spook is a friend. He'll float in the air just for me."

Slowly draw your fingers away. The ghost floats in midair between your extended palms.

It tries to fly away. Catch it in midair. It continues to float up and down at your command.

The secret of the floating ghost is a combination of puppetry and prestidigitation.

The floating ghost has a hole in the back of its head just big enough for the tip of your thumb to fit inside.

Since your thumb is hidden behind the ghost, it

SIDE
VIEW

appears as if the ghost is floating between your hands (see illustration).

Make it rise and fall by moving both hands alongside. Make it seem to fly away by quickly extending both hands and then "catching" the ghost with your fingertips.

Switch the hand that puts its thumb in the back of the ghost and make it float again. This will reduce suspicion about what's *really* happening.

Practice in front of a mirror until the "floating" action appears mysterious, but natural.

(Instructions for making your own "Floating Ghost" appear in Chapter 7, "Spooky Props.")

The Vanishing Ghost Box

Once the Floating Ghost has finished cavorting in the air, hold it in your left hand. Point to a small wooden box with your right hand.

Say: "When ghosts become too restless, they have to be put someplace for safekeeping."

Open the top lid of the box. Say: "This box has been specially lined with anti-ethereal dust to prevent our little spook from getting out."

Reach into your pocket and pretend to sprinkle some dust from it into the box. Then put the Floating Ghost inside. Close the lid and fasten it.

Pick the box up and hold it in front of you.

Say: "Spirits are awfully tricky, though. Sometimes they'll get away no matter what you do."

Pull the front and back doors open at the same time.

To everyone's surprise, the ghost is gone. The box is completely empty.

You can put your hand all the way through just to prove it!

The Vanishing Ghost Box has front and back doors that open in opposite directions. There is a secret pocket inside the box attached to the back door. When you put the Floating Ghost inside the box, you slip it into this secret pocket.

When you open the back door, the pocket remains

attached. It is hidden behind the door from the view of the audience (see illustration).

When performing "The Vanishing Ghost Box," pull the opposing doors open very quickly with a clean, sudden motion. The effect will be extremely startling.

(Plans for building "The Vanishing Ghost Box" appear in Chapter 7, "Spooky Props.")

Apparition in the Dark

The lights go out. The room is dark. Suddenly the glowing figure of a ghost appears from nowhere and begins to dance in the gloom.

Just as suddenly, it disappears into thin air.

Where did it *come* from? Where did it *go*?

It came from your pocket, and that's where it went, too.

Take a piece of heavy black material about 2 × 4 feet (60cm × 1.2m) and paint the picture of a scary ghost on it with glow-in-the-dark paint.

Make a hem along the top of the material and slip two 12-inch-long (30cm) sticks inside.

Expose the picture to a *very* bright light for a few hours before you are going to use it.

Fold the picture in half, roll it up and put it in your pocket.

To make the ghost appear, suddenly turn out the lights (or, if you're on a camp-out, sneak into the trees just beyond the campfire), unroll the picture and open it up.

The ghost will seem to appear from nowhere!

Move the top of it up and down.

The ghost will appear to dance.

Close it up, and the ghost disappears.

Try it. It's really fun.

Note: Glow-in-the-dark, or luminous, paint is readily available at most craft stores.

2. The Immaterial

Ghosts can pass through solid objects, that's why you can never catch one. Are they immaterial, or are haunted places simply full of holes?

Here are a group of spooky solid-through-solid effects whereby you can prove that in the realm of the spirits, nothing is as solid as it appears!

The Vanishing and Re-Appearing Wand

Open a plain, business-size envelope and take a black magic wand with white tips from inside it. Put the envelope on the table.

Say: "This magic wand belongs to the spirit of an old wizard. If we can hide it from him, it may give us spooky magic too."

Place the wand on a piece of newspaper and roll it inside.

Say: "I don't think the wizard will let us keep it, though."

Crumple the rolled newspaper tube and toss it over your shoulder.

Say: "I didn't think so."

Open the envelope on the table. The wand is back inside.

To prepare for this trick, make a magic wand by taking a short piece of dowel and painting it black with white tips.

Next, take a piece of black construction paper and roll the wand in it. Tape it tightly. Paint the tips of this construction paper tube white so it looks like the wand (1). Put the wand inside the tube, and place both inside the envelope.

When you open the envelope, take the paper tube wand out, but let the real wand remain in the envelope (2). Wrap the paper tube in the newspaper (3).

When you wad the newspaper (4), you're wadding the paper wand as well.

Take the real wand out of the envelope (5).

It will seem to have vanished from the newspaper and re-appeared in the envelope. Let everyone inspect the wand and the envelope if they want to.

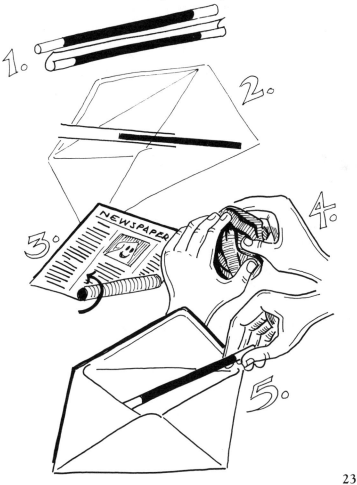

Wand Through the Hanky

Pick up an ordinary handkerchief and show it on both sides.

Say: "In a really haunted place, nothing is as solid as it looks."

Drape the handkerchief over your left fist and poke your right thumb into the center to make a small pocket. Take a short black magic wand with white tips (an ordinary pencil or pen will do) and stick it into the pocket in the center of the hanky.

Say: "This wand wouldn't be able to pass through the hanky in my hand unless the place were haunted."

Have a member of the audience push down on the top of the wand. At first it resists. Pass your right hand over the top of the wand a couple of times and then ask the spectator to push down on it again. This time it seems to slowly melt through the handkerchief.

Pull it free from the bottom.

Show the handkerchief again to prove there is no hole in it.

The secret of this trick lies in the way you make the pocket in the center of the handkerchief with your thumb.

To the audience, it looks as if you're poking your thumb straight down in the center of the hand-kerchief. What actually happens is that when your thumb presses downward, the forefinger and thumb of

24

your left hand underneath the handkerchief separate so that (1) the outside of the handkerchief is pressed against the inside of your left hand (2) your left forefinger and thumb pinch the hanky around your right thumb.

When you withdraw your thumb, it looks as if a pocket or depression has been left.

Push the wand into the depression (3), but hold the

little finger of your left hand (under the hanky) below it to keep it in place. Slowly release the pressure of your little finger. The wand will seem to melt through the handkerchief (4).

The Penetrating Key

Take an ordinary house key from your pocket and hold it up between the thumb and forefinger of your left hand.

Say: "Have you ever reached into your pocket and realized you lost your key? That's probably because a spook stole it. They can make keys go right through your clothes, and as you know, they love to play tricks on people."

Cover your left hand, along with the key, with a pocket handkerchief. Lift a corner of the handkerchief to show the audience that the key is underneath.

Flip the handkerchief back over it and then twist it around the key.

To everyone's amazement, the key will come right through the center of the handkerchief!

Let it fall free into the palm of your right hand, and then show the handkerchief to prove there isn't a hole in it.

There really isn't a hole in the center of the handkerchief, although that's what it really does look like to the audience.

Here's how it works:

Hold the key up between your right forefinger and thumb. Cover it with the hanky. Pinch the hanky between the edge of the key and your right thumb once it's covered (1).

After you flip the handkerchief back to show the audience that the key really is in the center (2), the

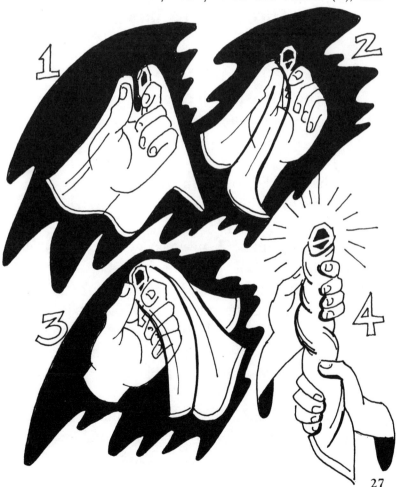

key will appear to be inside the fold—but since you've flipped the entire handkerchief forward, it's really hidden behind the hanky and is held in place by your thumb (3).

Twist the handkerchief until the key appears and falls from the top into the open palm of your right hand (4).

Through the Table

Place an ordinary key on a table beside a clear plastic tumbler.

Say: "Spooks love to pull pranks on people. One of their favorites is stealing your keys."

Put the tumbler over the key on the table. Put a sheet of newspaper over the tumbler and crumple it around the tumbler so it forms the same shape.

Say: "There's a ghost under this table. When I call him, he'll steal the key."

Hit the top of the newspaper-covered tumbler lightly with the flat of your right hand. Pick the tumbler up and draw it toward your body. The key is still on the table. Place the tumbler back over it.

Say: "I guess my friend the ghost didn't hear me."

Slap the top of the tumbler again. This time the newspaper crumbles flat on the table. Reach under the table.

Say: "I guess I must have startled him."

Bring the tumbler out from under the table.

Say: "He stole the tumbler instead."

The secret of this trick is in the newspaper.

When you form it around the tumbler, it assumes the tumbler's shape.

When you draw it toward your body to show that the key is still on the table, let the tumbler slip from under the newspaper onto your lap.

Put the newspaper back over the key. Since it still has the shape of the tumbler, everyone will think the tumbler is still wrapped in it.

Slap the newspaper flat and draw the tumbler, which is in your lap, from under the table.

Everyone will think the tumbler passed right through the table!

Tumbler Through Tumbler

Show two identical plastic tumblers.

Say: "You may think the idea of ghosts is one that doesn't hold water, but I can prove that you're wrong."

Pick up the tumblers in both hands and hold one over the other.

Say: "When the spirits are around, nothing holds anything."

Drop the top tumbler into the bottom tumbler.

Everyone will be stunned as it melts right through and falls to the table!

Just to prove that the tumbler is really immaterial, hold it by the fingertips of your left hand. Hold an identical tumbler over the top of it in your right hand. Drop the top tumbler into the bottom one. At the same time, release your grip on the bottom tumbler and catch the rim of the top one.

To your audience, it looks as if the top tumbler has fallen through the bottom one—proof positive that the tumbler is as immaterial as a ghost!

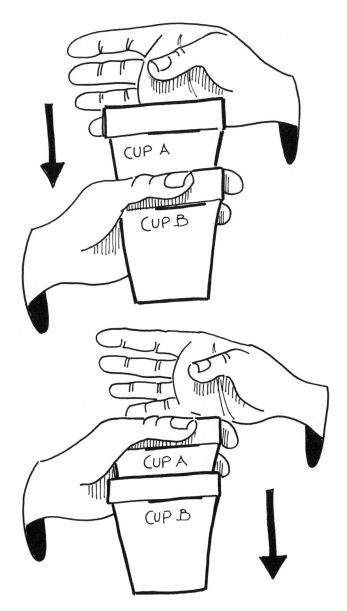

Remember, this is a quick effect, so dropping and catching the tumblers has to be perfectly timed to make it work.

Key Through the Tumbler

Hold a plastic tumbler in your left hand. In your right hand is a common house key. On a nearby table is a pocket handkerchief.

Say: "It's time for our friend the ghost to leave. He needs the key to the haunted house to get home."

Drop the key into the tumbler. Pick up the handkerchief and cover the tumbler with it.

Shift the tumbler from your left to your right hand.

Pull the handkerchief away and turn the tumbler over.

Nothing falls out. Show it to the audience. It's empty.

Say: "Good. I thought he'd never leave. But I'm glad he got his key."

Cut a hole in the bottom of the tumbler before beginning the trick. That way, when you drop the key inside, it falls through the hole and remains hidden in the palm of your hand.

When you shift the tumbler from one hand to the next, leave the hidden key in your palm and use this hand to pull the handkerchief from the top of the tumbler.

Everyone will think the key vanished.

Wrap the key in the handkerchief and put both in your pocket.

Leave your audience thinking that the ghost "spir-ited' it away!

The Disappearing Tumbler

A large cardboard box (or, better yet, a top hat) rests on a table. Show a drinking tumbler to the audience and place it inside.

Say: "Sometimes it's hard to get a drink when the spooks are around. They'll steal it from you if they see it."

Show the audience a black scarf; then cover the opening of the box with it. Reach inside and take the glass, with the scarf covering it, from inside.

Say: "Sometimes even hiding it doesn't help, though."

Toss the scarf-covered tumbler into the air. Catch the corner of the scarf and give it a snap.

To everyone's surprise, the tumbler has vanished!

The trick to this sudden and startling disappearance is in the scarf.

Cut a circle out of stiff cardboard the same diameter as the mouth of the tumbler (1). Paste it to the center of the scarf (2).

Place it over the box once the tumbler is inside. Grip the cardboard circle, and lift the scarf out, leaving the tumbler inside. It will look as if the tumbler is under the scarf (3).

For an added touch, particularly if you want to use the tumbler for another trick, tell the audience the ghosts put the tumbler back in the box once you've made it vanish.

Walk back over to the box and pull it out to prove the ghosts did put it back.

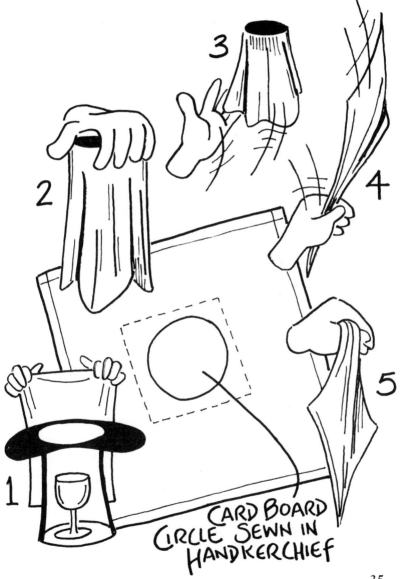

CARD BOARD
CIRCLE SEWN IN
HANDKERCHIEF

Full of Holes

Roll a piece of paper into a tube. Show it to a friend.

Say: "Ghosts could be all around, but you'd never know it. They can pass right through some people, because they're really full of holes only spirits can see. Are you full of holes? There's only one way to find out."

Hand him the tube and tell him to place it in front of his left eye. Tell him to hold his right palm beside the tube.

Sure enough, there seems to be a hole in the center of his hand.

This is more of an optical illusion than an actual trick. The hole appears because the left eye sees only the opening at the end of the tube. Because the right hand is held beside the tube, the hole seems to be in the middle of the right hand.

3. The Invisible Ghost

Have you ever heard the saying "Children should be seen and not heard"?

Most ghosts don't believe this. They believe they should be heard and not be seen.

The ghosts are invisible, but you can see the effects of their creepy manifestations. How else did that pencil move? By itself? And what other hand could have rung that bell and written that spooky message?

At least that's what your audience will think when it sees these mysterious illusions involving an invisible ghost.

Find the Ghost

You hold three cards. Their backs are blank. On one is the picture of a vampire. On the second is the picture of a ghost. On the third is a picture of a werewolf.

Say: "Ghosts are always shy. They're impossible to find if they feel like hiding. I'll bet you can't find this one."

Show the faces of the three picture cards to a spectator. The picture of the ghost is between the other two. Turn them over.

Say: "The ghost is in the center, right?"

Take it from between the other two pictures and place it facedown in front of you. Show the other two pictures.

Say: "The vampire and the werewolf are still here, so you must have found the ghost."

Turn the picture over, however, and everyone is in for a surprise. The ghost is no longer in it. All that's on the picture card is the simple word "Boo!"

The secret of this effect is in the three cards and the way you show them.

On one of the cards is a picture of a werewolf. On the second card is the word "Boo!" The third card has both the vampire and ghost's pictures. The vampire picture occupies the top half of this picture card, and

FRONT VIEW

SIDE VIEW

GIMMICK CARD

the picture of the ghost is near the bottom so its top appears about halfway down as shown in the illustration.

Show the backs of the picture cards separately,

spreading them from your right to your left hand. Square them in your left hand. Turn them over showing the full picture of the werewolf. Draw the werewolf and the "Boo" cards downwards together with your right hand, exposing both the vampire and ghost pictures. Your audience will think it is seeing the faces of all three picture cards, and it will believe the ghost is in the center.

Square the cards again and turn them facedown in your hand. Spread them and remove the center card (which has the word "Boo!" on its face) and place it facedown on the table. Turn the other two cards faceup and pull the werewolf picture down with your right hand—again exposing only the vampire face.

Square the two cards and put them aside.

Turn the "Boo!" card over for a laugh and a surprise.

The Ghost Writer

(The Spirit Slate and the Floating Pencil in the Bottle)

A small, blank writing slate is wrapped in a piece of newspaper.

Say: "Ghosts rarely speak, and they'll never let you see them. But they will answer riddles if you know how to ask them."

Place a bottle on top of the wrapped slate. Drop a pencil inside.

Ask: "Why are ghosts so lonely?"

Suddenly, the pencil mysteriously begins to rise, fall and dance inside the bottle. When it stops, you take the bottle away, rip open the newspaper, remove the slate and turn it over.

Written on its surface is the answer to the riddle: "Cause they ain't got no body."

The Spirit Slate

The secret is that the slate has a false front that lies loosely on the permanent surface, covering the written message. The false front is the same size as the face of the slate. The front of it is blank, and the back is covered with printed newspaper.

You show the slate to the audience with the false cover in place. People will see it as a blank writing slate. You place it facedown on a sheet of newspaper that is then wrapped around its back.

When you tear the newspaper wrapping away, the false front of the slate remains inside the wrapping.

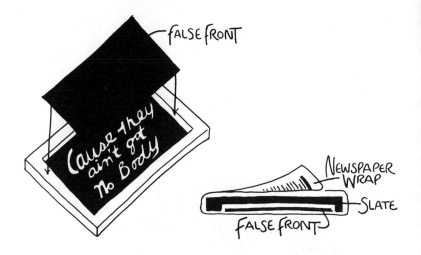

Since the reverse side of this loose flap has been covered with printed newspaper, it will blend against the newspaper wrapping and remain unnoticed.

The slate is turned faceup, and the message is found on its surface.

(For instructions on preparing a "Spirit Slate" see Chapter 7, "Spooky Props.")

The Floating Pencil

Attach a long piece of black thread to a button of your shirt. Make sure it is a dark-colored shirt. Against dark clothing the black thread will be practically invisible. Attach the other end of the thread to the eraser end of a pencil, securing it under an attachable rubber eraser.

Drop the pencil inside an open bottle. Moving your

body away from the bottle pulls on the thread, causing the pencil to rise. Moving your body toward the bottle makes it fall again.

To remove the ghostly pencil, drop your left hand behind the bottle, pulling on the thread and causing the pencil to rise to the top. Grasp it with your right hand and pull it out.

To perform this two-part effect, show the blank slate, wrap it in newspaper and place the empty bottle on top of it. Remove the pencil (with the secret thread already attached) from your shirt pocket and drop it in the bottle. Make it rise and fall. Remove it from the bottle, pull the thread free from the pencil and set the pencil aside. Unwrap the slate to reveal the message. Pass both around for inspection.

The audience will be amazed when it can discover no trickery!

The Noisy Poltergeist

Assemble a number of small items on a table including a small metal bell, a deck of playing cards, a wand or a pencil and a couple of different-colored balls. Hold a large handkerchief or a table napkin about 18 inches (45cm) square by the upper corners.

Say: "Poltergeists are noisy, and they like to throw things around. But they don't like to be seen because they're shy. You have to give them some privacy before they'll do their work."

Show both sides of the napkin, then hold it in front of the items on the table. Suddenly, cards start flying over the top of the napkin into the audience, followed by the balls. The bells begin mysteriously ringing. The pencil pokes over the top of the napkin. Then it flies over the top followed by the bell.

Pull the napkin away. There's absolutely nothing there.

Bend a pin into a hook and stick it into the left corner of the napkin. Show the front side of the napkin (1). Show the reverse side of the napkin by drawing the left corner toward your right shoulder while swinging your right arm in front of your left arm (2). Turn your body slightly to the left, and drape the napkin in front of the objects on the table so they are hidden from the audience. Pin the corner of the

napkin just below your armpit, holding it in place. This leaves your left hand free behind the napkin to toss objects over the top of it, ring the bell and so forth (3).

Your audience, however, won't know this. With a little practice, you'll make it look as if your left hand is really holding a corner of the napkin just as your right one is.

INTERIOR VIEW

The Rising Cards

Take out a deck of playing cards and, while shuffling them, say: "Ghosts and goblins love card tricks. And I have an invisible ghost who will help me do this one."

Have someone from the audience choose a card, show it to the rest of the audience and place it on top of the deck. Cut the cards and hold them vertically in your left hand with their faces toward the audience.

Say: "I didn't see which card you chose, but I don't have to. My ghostly friend will find it for me."

Place your right index finger on the top of the deck. Slowly raise your right hand.

The card that was chosen by the audience member slowly rises out of the pack with it!

The secret to this trick is to make certain the chosen card remains on the top of the deck.

Do this by using a move called "the false cut."

To work the false cut, hold the deck along the edges facedown between the thumb and fingers of your left hand. Grasp the *bottom* portion of the deck with your right hand, as the illustration shows, and cut away the bottom portion of cards.

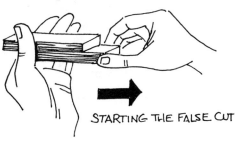

STARTING THE FALSE CUT

Tap them against the edge of the cards in your left hand. Then carry them over the top and place them on the table. Take the rest of the cards from your left hand and drop them on top of the cards on the table with your right hand.

This looks like a regular, innocent cut. But actually, you've re-assembled the deck exactly as it was to begin with. The chosen card is still facedown on the top of the deck.

FRONT VIEW   SIDE VIEW

Place the deck between the thumb and fingers of your left hand with the faces of the cards toward the audience. Hold it in front of you with the top of the deck tilted slightly toward your body.

As you place your right forefinger on top of the

48

deck, extend your little finger behind the deck so it touches the back of the chosen card.

As you lift your right hand, your little finger pushes the chosen card upwards.

As far as your audience is concerned, an invisible ghost is making it rise.

One-Handed Rising Cards

Here's another method of making a chosen playing card rise from the deck using only one hand.

Once the chosen card is facedown on top of the deck (as in the previous effect), lay the deck long-ways in the crook of your left hand with the faces toward the audience and your thumb against the back of the deck.

Hold your right hand over the top of the deck and gesture as if you were pulling on an invisible string. At the same time, push the top card upwards with your left thumb.

It will appear to the audience that its freely chosen card has been magically pulled from the deck.

The Spirit's Dowry
(or The Invisible Coins in the Paper Bag)

Hold up a paper lunch bag and show that it is completely empty.

Say: "Spooks and spirits usually don't carry any money because, like they say, you can't take it with you. But every now and then they need to scare up a few dollars like this."

The bag drops an inch or so as if something has suddenly landed inside it, and there is the sound of a coin striking its interior.

Hold the bag up again. Catch three or four more coins. Each is heard striking the inside of the bag.

Say: "Unfortunately, ghost money isn't worth very much. In fact, it's worth nothing at all."

Turn the bag over so the audience can see inside. It is completely empty.

Say: "Oh, well, easy come, easy go."

The secret to this trick is simple, but it takes a lot of practice in front of a mirror to make it look convincing.

Clutch the sack at the top with your left hand and support it at the bottom with your right. Each time you pretend to catch a coin, let the bag drop an inch or so, and flick the bottom part of it with your right middle finger.

By letting your left hand drop a little, it will look as if you've caught something. When you flick the bottom of the bag, it will sound as if something landed inside.

The Invisible Touch

How do you know if there's an invisible ghost in the room?

You can't see it.

But sometimes you can feel its invisible touch.

Have a volunteer sit in a chair facing you.

Say: "There's a ghost in the room. I know, because he's my friend. He's shy, so he won't let you see him. But he might let you know he's here if you don't look."

Point both your index fingers at your volunteer's eyes.

Say: "I have to make sure you don't peek."

Have her close her eyes. She will feel your fingers lightly touch them.

A second passes.

Suddenly, she is startled when someone—or something—touches her shoulders and tousles her hair.

Her eyes flash open. She looks around.

But there's nobody there!

The secret of "The Invisible Touch" is simple.

Your volunteer sees both your index fingers pointing toward her eyes before she closes them, so she thinks both of them touch her closed eyes. What she won't know is that after her eyes are closed, you lightly touch them with the index and middle finger of only your left hand.

Your right hand is free. It is that hand that touches her shoulder and tousles her hair!

The Ghostly Omelet

What do ghosts like to eat when their invisible stomachs start to rumble? No, not boo-berry pie—they like light, fluffy omelets.

At least that's what you explain to your audience as

you display a large mixing bowl covered with a linen table napkin.

Pick up the napkin by its corners and turn it around to show both sides. Cover the bowl with it again, and pick it up at the edge closest to you. Take hold of the edges of the napkin so that it now forms a bag.

Tip it toward the bowl. Suddenly to everyone's surprise, an egg rolls from the bag into the bowl.

Repeat this action until two or three eggs have rolled into the bowl.

Remove the napkin and set it aside.

Pretend to mix the eggs in the bowl.

Pick the bowl up, and tip it toward the audience as if you are throwing its contents at them.

To their amazement, the bowl is completely empty.

Say: "Well, I told you they like their omelets light and fluffy!"

Although you seem to produce three or more eggs, there's actually only one involved in this trick. This egg is plastic, and there is a long black thread glued to the end of it. The other end of the thread is sewn to the center edge of the napkin.

At the beginning of the trick, the egg is in the bowl. The napkin is held over the bowl with the thread at the lower edge. Show both sides of the napkin by lifting the opposite edges (1).

After showing the napkin, spread it over the bowl

with the thread toward your body (2). Pick up the napkin by the center edge where the thread is attached (3). This will draw the egg out of the bowl into the center of the napkin.

Form the napkin into a bag (4) and pour it into the bowl.

Repeat the procedure to produce more eggs.

When you've produced enough—usually three or four will do—take the napkin and the egg out of the bowl, wad them into a ball and set them aside.

The audience will be startled when you throw the contents of the bowl out, since there really isn't anything in it!

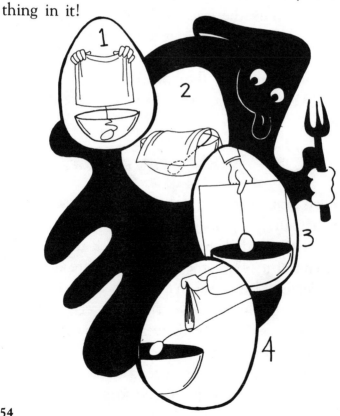

4. Floating Stuff

When restless spooks are wandering, nothing seems to stay put.

Gravity itself no longer has any meaning as playful spirits make things rise and float about, supported by only their invisible fingers.

But ghosts aren't the only ones who can make things rise in the air. You can do it too, once you've learned the secrets of these simple levitations!

Knife Levitation

Take an ordinary butter knife and place it on the open, extended palm of your right hand. Press your thumb against it. Explain that if you concentrate, the power of the invisible spirits will keep it from falling.

Grip your wrist with your left hand.

Say: "I have to keep my hand perfectly steady to make the magic work."

Turn your right hand over, still holding the knife against your palm with your thumb. Slowly release your thumb.

The knife remains suspended in midair beneath it.

The secret to the knife levitation is simple but very effective.

Grip your right wrist with your left hand (1).

When you turn your right hand over, extend the index finger of your left hand so it touches the knife (2).

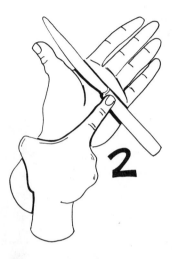

When you release your thumb, your index finger keeps it against your palm. To your audience, however, the knife will seem to be suspended in midair.

The Rising Ring

Take a ring off one of your fingers and let everyone inspect it. Say: "This is a ring that all ghosts like. They'd steal it if they could."

Take a pencil with an eraser fixed to its end from your pocket. Place the ring over the top.

Say: "One of the ghosts is trying to steal it now!"

To everyone's surprise, the ring begins to climb up and down the pencil by itself.

The rising ring trick works the same way as "The Floating Pencil" illusion described on page 42.

Attach a piece of black thread to a button on your shirt or jacket. Secure the other end of it to the pencil by placing it under the eraser on the tip (an ink pen with a removable cap will work as well).

Drop the ring over the top of the pencil and the thread. As you extend your hand away from your body, the thread will pull the ring upwards.

Floating Cards

Place your right hand palm down on a table. Slip two playing cards beneath it. Place two more on the sides of these, then four more on the four corners.

Lift your hand slowly.

All eight cards rise into the air with it.

Knock them all off with your left hand.

Make your right hand into a fist. Then open it and show that your palm is empty.

Explain that it was a ghostly hand that held the cards against it.

To make this trick work, wear a ring on your right hand. Place a toothpick under it.

Place the first two cards under the toothpick (1). The toothpick will support the cards. Place the rest of the cards under your hand on top of the first two (2).

After you knock the cards free, making your right hand into a fist will break the toothpick. Shake your hand to get rid of the pieces.

That way, when you show your empty hand, there won't be a clue remaining as to what made the cards rise with it.

A Floating Scarf

Take a scarf out of your pocket.

Say: "Ghosts love scarves. They carry them every-where. You can always tell when ghosts are around because they'll climb inside a scarf and make it float with them!"

Grip the scarf in your upturned, closed fist, and draw it about halfway through.

Turn your hand over and open your fist.

The scarf remains suspended in thin air beneath it!

The secret gimmick that makes this trick work is a simple, flesh-colored rubber band.

Stretch the rubber band under your hand between your thumb and little finger (1).

Pull the scarf under the rubber band (2).

Clench your fist around it and turn your hand over. Pull the scarf halfway through your fist. Turn your hand over and open your fist.

Since the scarf is under the rubber band, it will seem to be magically suspended under your hand (3)!

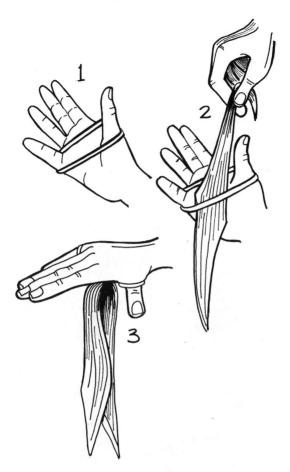

The Ghostly Touch

Place a pencil on a table. Explain that the spirits have given you the power of the ghostly touch.

Place the tips of your fingers on top of the pencil. Raise your hand.

The pencil remains suspended on your fingertips!

While it looks to the audience as if your fingertips are merely touching the pencil, actually they're gripping it.

Place your index and little finger on the side of the pencil, and your ring and middle fingers on the top—but slightly over the edge—as in the illustration. Your ring and middle fingers press the pencil against your index and little fingers, holding the pencil in place.

5. Are You Psychic?

Bat

They say only "sensitive" people can hear and see the spirits that roam the night.

They say those "sensitive" people are psychic: They have ESP—*extrasensory perception.*

It's said that psychic people can predict the future,

and that they can tell you what you're thinking about *while* you're thinking about it.

Are you psychic?

Do you have ESP?

Here are some illusions that will convince your audience that you do!

The Tell-Tale Timepiece

Pull out a scroll and unroll it on a table.

On the scroll is the picture of a clock.

Say: "Ghosts are restless, but they are always on time. They are going to appear at an exact hour."

Arbitrarily point to someone.

Say: "The spirits will tell you exactly when."

Ask that person to merely *think* of an hour pictured on the clock.

Pick up a pencil. Say you are going to tap the pencil point on the numbers of the clock. Tell your volunteer to count as you tap, starting with the number he thought of and adding one to that number.

For example, if your subject chooses the number seven on the clock, he will add one to the number and mentally count "eight" the first time the pencil point hits the clock. He'll then count "nine," "ten," and so forth.

Tell him to say "Stop" when he *mentally* reaches 20.

He, and everyone else watching, will be amazed when your pencil point is on the hour the volunteer thought of the instant he cries "Stop!"

Sounds impossible?

The ghosts say boo to that!

All you have to do is remember the number seven.

When you start tapping, tap the pencil point at random all over the clock until you reach seven. After reaching the number seven—on the eighth tap—place the pencil point on 12, and continue tapping counter-clockwise until the volunteer says "Stop."

If your volunteer can count—and is honest—your pencil point will rest on the hour he chose every time.

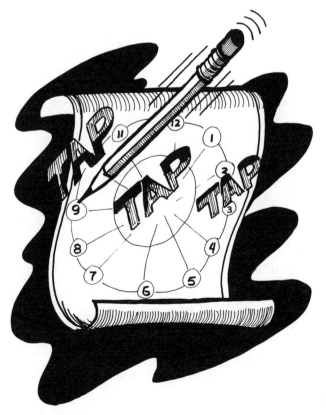

The Foolproof Prediction

This is a mental effect that can't possibly miss. Begin by asking people from the audience to call out their first names. Write each one down on a separate slip of paper.

Ask for proper spellings as you write.

Once you've finished writing a name, fold the slip of paper and drop it into a paper bag.

When all the names are in the bag, mix them all up. Then have someone from the audience reach inside and take out one of the slips. Discard the bag and ask the person who drew the slip to hold it, folded, in front of her.

After mentally straining for a moment, call out a name.

Have the person holding the slip unfold it and show it to the rest of the audience.

All will be startled to find the name you called written on the slip of paper.

This trick seems like a mental miracle, but the secret is incredibly simple. While you pretend to write down all the names called from the audience, you actually write only one—the first name called—on *all* the slips of paper. If the first name called is "Brian," for example, you write "Brian" on every slip.

That way it doesn't matter which slip is taken out of the bag, because they all say the same thing.

The only reason you ask people to spell their names as you write is to misdirect them into thinking you are writing all the names down and not just one of them.

Make sure to get rid of the bag once the slip is selected by an audience member, though. That way no one will ask to see what's written on the *other* slips!

The Card Prediction

Write the name of a playing card on a piece of paper and seal it in an envelope.

Explain that if the spirits are agreeable, they will grant you the power to predict the future.

Hand a deck of cards to a spectator and have him select one, but don't touch the deck while he's doing it.

Have him show the card to everyone else.

Have a second person tear open the envelope and read your prediction.

To everyone's amazement, the card the spectator holds is the exact same card you wrote down *before* it was selected!

The secret of this mind-boggling feat is to make one of the spectators pick a card that you already know. This is known as "forcing" a card, and it's simple to do.

First, look at the card on the top of the deck and remember what it is.

Square the deck and put it aside.

Write the name of the top card on a piece of paper and seal it in an envelope.

After you've done that, ask a volunteer to think of a number between one and ten. Let's say he chooses the number seven. Tell him you want him to deal six cards off the top of the deck and then look at the seventh card.

While explaining this, deal seven cards yourself facedown on the table, as if you are demonstrating what you want them to do.

This places the top card—say, the six of spades—seven cards from the top. Perform the false cut described in "The Rising Cards" (pages 47–48) and hand the deck to the volunteer.

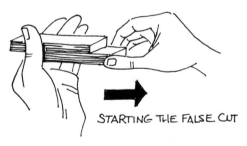

STARTING THE FALSE CUT

Performing the false cut will leave him believing that the seven cards you dealt to demonstrate what you wanted him to do are now somewhere in the center of the deck.

Since you don't actually touch the deck while the card is being selected, and since someone else tears open the envelope, no one will ever suspect trickery.

Mind Reading

Here's another trick that will convince your audience you have ESP.

Hand four sheets of paper and four envelopes to four different volunteers from the audience.

Ask the volunteers to write different messages—the name of a friend; a favorite color; a favorite movie; a special place—and seal them in the envelopes.

By pressing each of the envelopes against your forehead one at a time, you will amaze everyone by announcing exactly what is written inside before opening the envelopes up.

This trick is actually an expansion of "The Foolproof Prediction" on page 66.

First, ask for names from the audience just as in "The Foolproof Prediction." Write "Brian" (or whatever name) on all the slips. Once all the names are in the bag, hand out four envelopes to different members of the audience.

Hand three of the volunteers slips of paper like the ones you used.

Tell one of the volunteers to write the name of his favorite movie on his slip and seal it in his envelope.

Tell the second volunteer to write the name of her favorite place on her slip and seal it in her envelope.

Tell the third volunteer to write his favorite color on his slip and seal it in his envelope.

Have the fourth volunteer take one of the slips from the bag. Have her look at the name on it, show it to the others, and then seal it in her envelope.

Collect all the envelopes once the volunteers have finished.

Pretend to mix up the envelopes, but secretly make sure the one containing the name pulled from the bag is on the bottom of the stack.

Pick up the first envelope and press it to your forehead. Say: "Ah ha! The name you chose from the bag is Brian (or whatever name has been written on all the slips in the bag)!"

Tear open the envelope and pretend to read the message inside. Say: "Sure enough, the name is Brian."

Read to yourself what is *actually* written on the paper. Let's say it's the color one of the others wrote. Lay the slip aside and lift the *second* envelope to your forehead. Tell everyone that *this* envelope contains the name of the color.

Do this until you get to the last envelope. Since you tell them it contains the message you secretly read from the last envelope you opened, your audience will never know it really contains a name you knew from the start, and it will never know just how it's been tricked!

Mind Reading II

Here's another way of doing the Mind Reading trick.

Pass out three pieces of paper and three envelopes. Ask the first volunteer to write a color, the second a friend's name and the third a favorite movie.

Pick a fourth person and force a card just as in "The Card Prediction" on page 67.

While the volunteer is dealing out the "forced" card, write *your* prediction on a piece of paper and place it in an envelope.

Make sure the envelope containing your prediction is on the bottom of the four. Then proceed to predict and open the envelopes, as in "Mind Reading."

The Deck Exchange

Begin with two decks of cards. Hand one of them to a participant sitting opposite you. Tell the person to select a card, remember it, put it on top of the deck and cut the deck once.

Exchange decks. Tell the person you're going to read her mind and find the card she chose.

Unfortunately, you can't. Get a little upset, stating that she isn't concentrating hard enough.

Have her select another card, place it on top of the deck, cut deck once and exchange with you again.

Tell her to *really* concentrate this time.

After a moment of mental straining, you are able to pull the card she is thinking of from the deck!

Failing to find psychically the card your victim selected the first time is simple mis-direction. The secret of this trick is to take a peak at the bottom card of the first deck of cards you exchange. That way, when your volunteer selects a card the second time, the bottom card of your original deck will be placed directly on top of it.

When the deck is returned to you, all you have to do is find the card you remembered. The card directly in front of it will be the selected card.

With a touch of acting and a dash of drama, everyone watching—including the person who selected the card—will be convinced that you found it using psychic powers.

The Haunted Pendulum

Here's a spooky stunt that's fun to do while sitting around with friends.

Tie a ring to about a foot or so of string. Hold the string by the end so the ring hangs down like a pendulum.

Tell everyone that the ring is haunted, and that the spirit it holds will answer questions.

Have a volunteer hold his hand, palm up, under the ring. Have him ask a yes-or-no question.

The pendulum will swing back and forth for yes, and it will swing in a circle for no.

Actually, just thinking yes or no sets up the vibrations in your fingers that changes the direction of the pendulum, so there's nothing to it.

But it's a pretty nifty effect, nonetheless.

The Mysterious Lights

Show your audience a cardboard folder cut and decorated to look like a haunted house. Point out the three windows in the front of it.

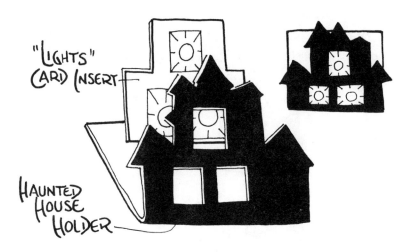

"LIGHTS" CARD INSERT

HAUNTED HOUSE HOLDER

Take out three cards from inside. Each has three "lights" in different colors. The "lights" can be seen through the "Haunted House" windows.

The first card has yellow lights, the second has red lights and the third has blue lights.

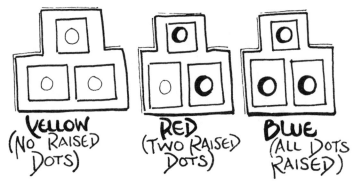

YELLOW
(NO RAISED DOTS)

RED
(TWO RAISED DOTS)

BLUE
(ALL DOTS RAISED)

Hand the Haunted House and the lights cards to someone in the audience.

Turn your back and tell him to put any color lights he likes in the Haunted House.

Tell him to put the Haunted House in your hands.

Turn back around, smile and tell him the exact color he chose.

Bring the Haunted House from behind your back.

Sure enough, the lights in its windows are the color you predicted.

"The Mysterious Lights" works by sense of touch.

Instead of drawing three green lights on the green card, cut a small circle out of cardboard (1) the same size as the other two and paste it on the card so it shows through the right-hand window of the Haunted House.

Draw all three "lights" on the yellow card.

Paste two dots and draw one light on the red card.

Paste three dots on the blue card.

When the Haunted House is handed to you behind your back, feel how many dots there are.

If you feel no dots, the color is yellow. If you feel two dots, the color is red. If you feel three dots, the lights are blue.

6. Spooky Magic with Creepy Creatures

The night is dark and the air is alive with the peal of distant thunder. Faceless creatures reach for you from the darkness and fog.

Bats fly. Spiders spin. Rats skitter down empty hallways.

The children of the night are restless. Can magic force them to do your bidding? Of course it can!

Here's a handful of spooky tricks that are sure to make you Master of the Dark!

Bats in the Belfry

Show a large, white rectangular card, holding it in your right hand. There is a small picture of a bat in the center.

Say: "There are a lot of bats around a creepy place like this, and keeping count of them isn't easy."

Then turn the card around and say, "I've only seen one bat today, but I saw four of them yesterday." There are four bats on the other side of the card.

Say: "I expected to see at least three bats by now," and then turn the card around again. There are three bats showing on the card.

Say: "Tomorrow I hope to see six bats." Turn the card over. Sure enough, there are six bats on the card.

Turn the card around again and say: "But for now, there's just one."

Once again there is only a single bat in the center of the card!

While it *appears* that the card has four sides, one with a single bat, one with four bats, another with three bats and the final with six bats, it really has only two sides.

One side of the card has two bats on it—one in the center and another beside it near the edge. The other side has five bats—a row of three bats along the top and two bats below with a blank space between them (1).

FIGURE 1

To make the illusion work, begin by holding your right-hand fingers together against the front of the card with your thumb against the back. On the first side of the card, the fingers of your right hand cover the bat near the edge (2). All the audience sees is the bat in the center and the blank space to the left of it. It looks as if there is only one bat.

Turn the card around by gripping the lower middle edge from behind with your left hand (3). The fingers of your left hand cover the bat in the row of three. The audience sees four bats (4).

78

When your turn the card again, you cover the blank space near the edge. Both bats on the front side are showing, but spectators will assume there is a third bat under your fingertips (5).

The same is true of the next turn with your left hand (6). Your fingers cover the blank space between the left and right bats beneath the row of three. All five bats are visible, but since your fingers cover the blank space, it looks as if there are six bats showing (7).

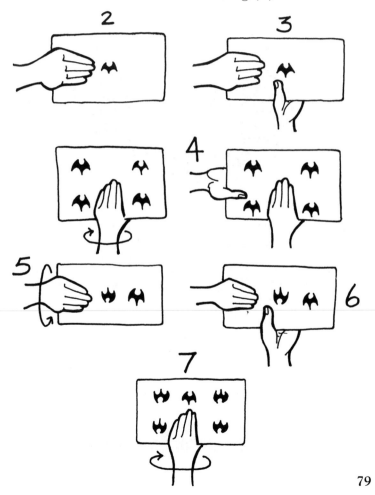

While this strange type of multiplication would drive a math teacher *batty*, the moves are simple: Turn your wrist so your fingers are toward you, grip the card from behind and twist your wrist again to turn the card away from you toward your audience. Your left hand grips the card along the middle of the long edge and turns it around; your right hand grips the end and turns it over.

The Bat's Cage

Hold up a small wooden box covered with a black cloth.

Say: "I have a pet bat. He lives in here."

Lift the cover up to show the inside of the box, which is seen to be completely empty.

Put the cover back over the opening.

Say: "My pet bat is named Spooky. He's a vampire bat, and he only comes out when he's hungry."

Flash a slightly sinister smile and say: "It's feeding time, Spooky!"

Lift the cloth cover again.

The audience will be startled to see a black vampire bat leering at them from inside the box!

The secret of "The Bat's Cage" is in the box itself. The box is perfectly square and open at the front and back. There is a mirror placed diagonally from the top of the front to the back of the bottom (1). The mirror reflects the side of the box, making it appear as if the entire box is empty.

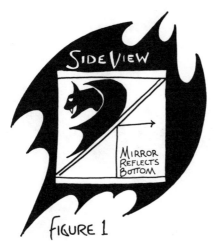

FIGURE 1

The vampire bat is attached to the other side of the mirror, which is covered with red felt.

To perform the trick, start with the box in your left hand with your body turned slightly to the left. Lift the cover with your right hand, showing the supposedly "empty" mirrored side of the box (2).

Replace the cover and transfer the box to your right hand, turning the box around and shifting your body to the right as you do (3).

As you lift the cover to expose the bat, extend your left hand slightly so that it looks as if the bat is beginning to lunge (4).

Your audience will be startled every time!

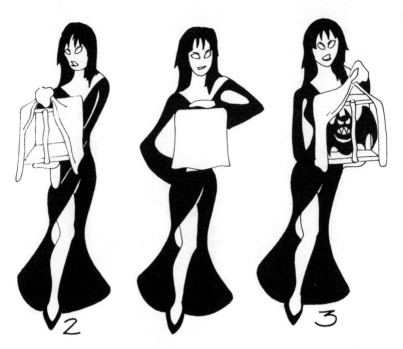

(Instructions for making your own "Bat's Cage" appear in Chapter 7, "Spooky Props.")

The Thing in the Box
(A Three-Part Trick)

1: The Locked Door

On a table is a pad of paper, a pencil and a closed wooden box.

Say: "A lot of spooks live in haunted houses. But you can't see them if you can't get inside."

Take the pencil and draw a picture of a closed door

on the top sheet of the pad. Show your picture around, then fold it in half and pull it off the pad.

Say: "There's only one way to open the door to the haunted house, and that's with a key."

Take a key out of your pocket. Hand it to a spectator and have him press it against the folded picture.

Have him unfold the picture. To everyone's surprise, the drawing of the door on the sheet of paper is now wide open!

Before you show this trick, draw the picture of the *open* door on the second sheet of the pad (1). Fold the picture in half underneath the first sheet (2).

Draw the picture of the closed door on the top sheet while spectators watch. Fold in half.

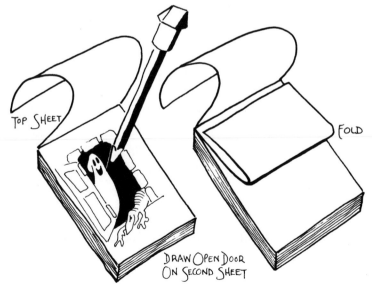

TOP SHEET

FOLD

DRAW OPEN DOOR
ON SECOND SHEET

Pick up the pad and turn the back of it to the audience. Pretend to tear off the top sheet, but really tear out the second sheet (3). Set the pad facedown on the table, and place the box on top of it. This will prevent spectators from turning it over.

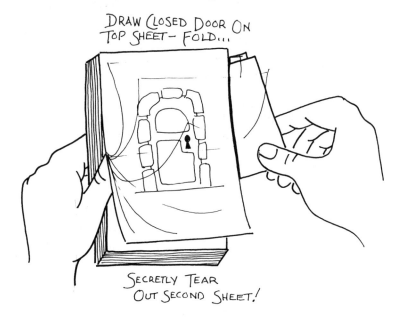

DRAW CLOSED DOOR ON TOP SHEET— FOLD...

SECRETLY TEAR OUT SECOND SHEET!

2: The Vanishing Key

Place the key on top of the picture of the open door. Say: "You need the key to the haunted house to get inside. But just because you have it now doesn't mean the creatures who live inside are going to let you keep it."

As your spectators watch, wrap the key into a package using the picture of the open haunted house door. Once the key is wrapped, hand the packet to someone in the audience.

Say: "We'll see if the spooks want you to go inside."

Tell your innocent "victim" to tear the packet open.

Everyone will be amazed to find it's absolutely empty!

The secret of this trick is in the folding.

Fold the picture around the key, as shown in the illustration. While it looks as if you've secured the key inside the wrapper, you've actually left one end open.

Let the key slide into your hand as shown, and then palm it in your right hand.

Once you've handed the packet to a spectator, casually put your hand in your pocket, leaving the key there.

3: The Thing in the Box

Once the key has vanished from the folded picture say, in a startled voice: "The ghosts have stolen the key! That means they don't want us in the haunted house. We'll have to ask them nicely to give it back."

Turn to the box on top of the pad. Knock on the top of it. Say: "We'd really like the key back."

Try to lift the lid. It won't budge. Look at your audience, smile and say: "I seem to have forgotten the magic word."

Turn back to the box and say: "Please?"

Lift the lid. A monstrous hand rises from the inside.

Tied around its bony fingers is the key!

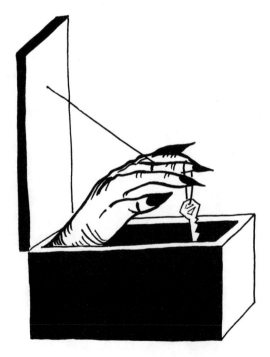

"The Thing in the Box" is a nifty prop, and it makes a terrific conclusion to this three-part trick. The box is just big enough to hold the monster hand, which is hinged at the back and lifted by a thread attached inside the lid. When you open the lid of the box, the thing rises automatically from inside.

Before beginning the trick, attach a duplicate key to the fingers of the thing.

After knocking on the top of the box, *pretend* that it won't open. Really act as if it's locked and won't budge.

When you finally open the box, the thing will come out, and it will be holding the duplicate key.

(*Instructions for making "The Thing in the Box" appear in Chapter 7, "Spooky Props."*)

The Creature Bag

Show a black, cloth bag. Turn it inside out to prove it's empty.

Say: "Creepy creatures show up all the time in the haunted house, usually when you least expect them."

Have someone reach inside the bag. It's still empty. Flash a sinister smile and have him reach inside again.

When his hand comes out of the bag, it's holding a spider!

Take the spider from him.

Say: "Where did that come from?"

Put it back in the bag. Drop the bag on the floor and step on it. Say: "There, that should do it."

Have someone else reach inside the bag.

There isn't a spider inside.

This time, there's a rat!

The cloth bag has a secret pocket that allows small objects to be held in the upper corner and then dropped inside (see illustration).

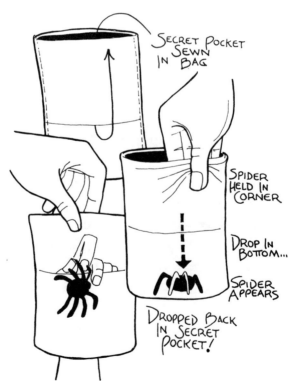

To work the bag, place the spider and the rat inside and hold them in the corner under your hand. When your volunteer reaches inside, he'll feel nothing. Release the spider and it falls inside the bag.

Hold the bag upside down by the bottom. The rat will stay in the upper corner. Take the spider and put it inside the bag, dropping it into the secret pocket.

Grip the upper edge of the bag, holding the spider and the rat. Drop the bag on the ground. Step on it in the middle.

Pick it up by the upper edge again. Hold the spider in place. Let the rat drop in the bag.

Everyone will think the bag is overrun with creepy creatures!

(To make "The Creature Bag" and the creepy creatures, see Chapter 7, "Spooky Props." The instructions appear there.)

The Haunted House

Set an open-ended box with a tube (a tin can will do) inside it on a table. The box is painted to look like the outside of a spooky old house. It has an open door in the front. The tube is decorated to look like a brick chimney. The chimney is visible through the open door of the box.

Lift the box, leaving the tube on the table, and show that it's completely empty. Put it back and take the tube from the inside. Show that it, too, is hollow and empty.

Spectators can see through the open door that the box is still empty.

Say: "This little house is like all haunted houses.

The ghosts are there, but you can't see them. At least, not without some spooky magic."

Wave your hands over the top of the chimney and say: "Hear my words and heed them well! Beckon to my secret spell!"

Reach inside. Suddenly, from the top of the chimney, out fly a bunch of bats followed by a couple of creepy spiders, a handful of scarves and, finally, a small skeleton!

The secret of the haunted house is a canister inside the "chimney" tube that holds the bats, spiders, scarves and other items. Since it is covered with nonreflective black material, and the interior of the box is painted flat black as well, the canister remains invisible inside the box once the tube is removed.

Load the canister prior to showing "The Haunted House."

Once it's loaded, remove the box, leaving the tube, and show that it's empty (1). Lift the tube out of the box and show that it is empty as well (2). Put the tube back inside the box. Reach inside and pull out all the ghoulish goodies you've already loaded into the hidden canister (3).

To make the bats appear to "fly" from the top, place them on top of the other items inside and toss them lightly in the air.

For an extra dramatic touch, produce everything

BOX
TUBE

HIDDEN
CANISTER

I.   II.   III.

from the house but the skeleton. Pull the tube out of the box again to show there's nothing left inside. Put your hand through it to prove the point.

Then, after placing it back in the box, reach into the tube and pull out the skeleton.

(To build "The Haunted House," turn to Chapter 7, "Spooky Props.")

The Killer Tomato

Set two tin cans with both of their ends removed beside each other on a tabletop. One is an eight-ounce (240ml) tomato sauce can. The other is a 16-ounce (.47 l) tomato soup tin or whole-tomato can.

Say: "Some of the strangest movie monsters of all time were the Killer Tomatoes. Killer Tomatoes would jump off vines and roll out of the supermarket. Sometimes they'd come right out of the can to get you!"

Pick up the larger of the two tin cans and show that it's empty. Drop the smaller through it to prove the point, then show that the small one is empty too. Drop the smaller tin through the larger one again, and hold the smaller one in the palm of your hand.

Say: "Just because these tin cans are empty, it doesn't mean we're safe. Killer tomatoes are like ghosts. You never know where they'll show up."

Pluck the tin can from your palm.

There's a killer tomato resting on it!

Quickly toss it into the audience and watch them jump.

To produce "The Killer Tomato," fix a hook into a plastic tomato just big enough to fit inside the small tin can. Place the tomato inside with the hook on the upper edge (1) prior to showing the trick.

When you drop the small tin can through the larger one, the hook on the tomato will catch on the upper edge of the larger can (2).

Once the small tin can has fallen through the larger one, turn the larger one over in the palm of your hand so that the tomato is now on your palm.

Drop the small tin through the large one again (3), and lift it up and away, leaving the small can and the tomato on your palm.

When you remove the smaller can, the tomato will seem to have appeared out of nowhere!

7. Spooky Props

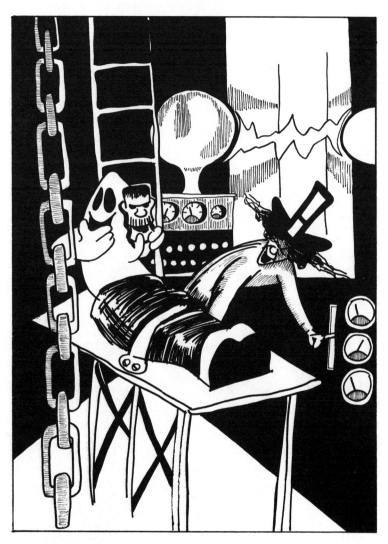

Got your tools and materials ready?

Then here are the instructions for the props and equipment you've read about in the past six chapters.

None of these props are hard to build.

Just follow these directions and soon, like Dr. Frankenstein, you'll find yourself crying, "It's alive!"

Gathering Materials

You can find most of the materials you need to build Spooky Props around the house or in a variety of stores, and most of them don't cost much.

Different-size rubber bats, skeletons, rats, spiders, monster-hand gloves and so forth can be found at party accessory stores, costume shops and magic shops, especially around Halloween.

You can buy cloth in any fabric store. Material is usually sold by the yard, but it is possible to buy smaller remnant pieces as well.

Paint, brushes, Styrofoam balls, fake plastic vegetables (such as the small tomato used in "The Killer Tomato"), plastic eggs, felt squares and filler material for stuffing are available at most craft and floral supply stores.

You can get poster board and construction paper at stationery and office supply stores.

Other materials such as nails, thumbtacks, white glue, hinges and fasteners can be found on the shelves of any hardware store.

Many of the props described in this chapter call for pieces of wood in special sizes. You can buy these at any home and garden or lumber store. Most of these places will cut wood to specific sizes for a very small, per-cut cost.

One of the illusions, "The Bat's Cage," calls for a small mirror. Any glass, mirror or window store will cut small pieces of mirror to your specifications for a few dollars.

You can find any and all of these shops and stores in a flash in the pages of your local telephone directory. Give them a call before heading out to shop. That will save you time and aggravation.

The Phantom Tube

To make a Phantom Tube, you'll need:
an empty 24-ounce juice can (.7 l juice tin)
a piece of stiff cardboard
2 identically colored plastic lids
flat black paint
white glue

Clean the tin can and remove the label. Use a can opener to remove *both* ends of the can. Using one of the can tops—(be careful—its edges are sharp!)—trace a circle on the cardboard and cut it out with a scissors (1).

Push the cardboard circle into the center of the tin can. It should fit snugly. Put a bead of white glue

97

around the outside of both sides of the cardboard circle (2).

Once the glue has dried, paint the inside of both chambers of the can flat black. This way the cardboard in the center of the can will not reflect any

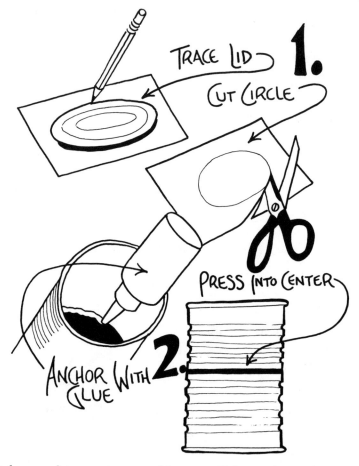

light, making it impossible to tell how deep the can really is.

Fix the plastic lids on the ends of the can, and there you have it.

The Floating Ghost

For "The Floating Ghost," you'll need:
a 2-inch (5cm) Styrofoam ball
an 18-inch (45cm) white handkerchief or scarf
a small piece of black felt
straight pins
white glue

Press your thumb into the ball to make a hole or depression deep enough so that the ball will stay on your thumb during the performance (1).

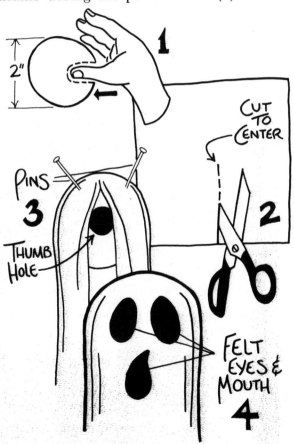

2"

1

CUT TO CENTER

PINS
3

THUMB HOLE

2

FELT EYES & MOUTH
4

99

Next, take a pair of scissors and make a single cut up the middle edge of the scarf to just below the center (2).

Drape the scarf over the ball with the cut over the hole (3).

Secure the scarf to the ball with straight pins.

Cut eyes and a mouth from the black felt, and glue them to the front of the ghost (4).

Note: Use a silk or rayon scarf for the shroud of "The Floating Ghost" if you intend to use the ghost in "The Phantom Tube." Silk or rayon is much less bulky than cotton or other material.

If you don't intend to use "The Floating Ghost" with "The Phantom Tube," an ordinary white handkerchief is fine for the shroud.

The Vanishing Ghost Box

For "The Vanishing Ghost Box," you'll need:
4 pieces of quarter-inch (4mm) plywood
    measuring 4 × 4½ inches (10 × 11.25cm)
2 pieces of quarter-inch plywood
    measuring 4 × 4 inches (10 × 10cm)
3 sets of small hinges
a hook-and-eye fastener
a single square of colored felt
an 8 × 11-inch (20 × 27.5cm) piece of cardboard
transparent tape
white glue

Glue and nail pieces A and B to piece C (1) to form the base of the box.

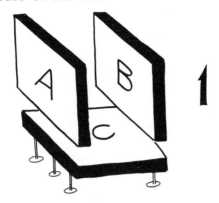

Attach the lid to the base with the first set of hinges. Attach the hook-and-eye fastener to the front of the lid (2).

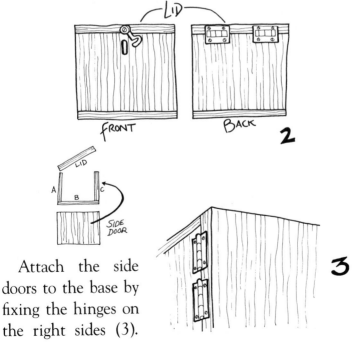

Attach the side doors to the base by fixing the hinges on the right sides (3).

Cut the cardboard and fold it into the shape of a box 3 inches (7.5cm) wide and 3 inches (7.5cm) deep (4).

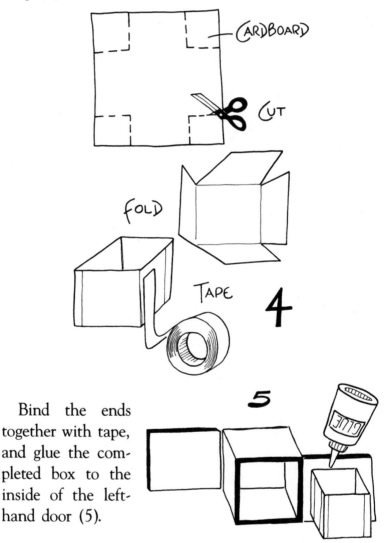

Bind the ends together with tape, and glue the completed box to the inside of the left-hand door (5).

Cover the inside of the base and the back of the right-hand door with colored felt.

Find the Ghost

Making a set of "Find the Ghost" picture cards is simple.

From a piece of stiff poster board, cut four pieces measuring 3 × 5 inches (75 × 125mm).

Draw the characters on the faces of three of the cards, dividing the surfaces in half, so that the upper half contains the face of the character and the lower half contains its upper torso (1).

Cut the lower two inches (5cm) off the picture of the ghost (which should remove the lower torso, leaving all of the face). Secure the ghost picture to the bottom of the vampire picture with tape (2).

When you show the cards, all three faces should be seen clearly.

Leave the fourth card blank, or decorate it with the word "Boo!," a question mark or some other symbol to indicate that the ghost has disappeared.

You can leave the backs of the picture cards blank or decorate them to suit your taste.

The Spirit Slate

For "The Spirit Slate," you'll need:
a piece of thin plywood measuring 4 × 4½ inches
    (10 × 11.25cm)
4 ice cream sticks
2 pieces of black poster board measuring about 4 × 3
    inches (10 × 7.5cm)
white paint
a sheet of newspaper
white glue

The larger piece of plywood is the base. Glue one of the pieces of black poster board to the top of it. This will be the surface of the slate with the message on it.

Glue the ice cream sticks to the base, forming a frame around the black poster board slate surface (1). Paint the ghost's message on the slate's surface (2).

The second piece of black poster board is used as the false front. Cut a piece from the newspaper sheet, preferably covered with type, and glue it to the back of the second piece of poster board (3).

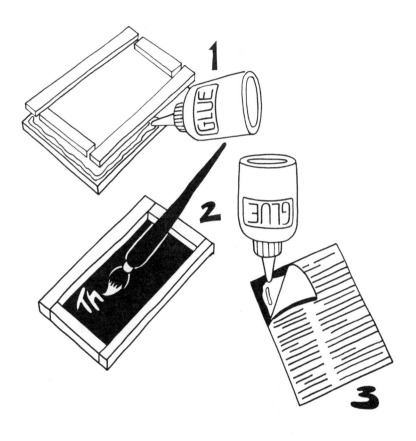

Note: Newspaper will yellow with time. If the newspaper backing on your false front has yellowed, it will show against a fresh newspaper sheet. Make a replacement before showing the trick.

Additional note: For a different look, use a piece of colorful gift wrap to wrap the slate in, using a piece of the same paper for the false cover.

The Bat's Cage

For "The Bat's Cage" you'll need:

2 pieces of quarter-inch (4mm) plywood
     measuring 5 × 6 inches (12.5 × 15cm)

2 pieces of quarter-inch plywood measuring
     6 × 6½ inches (15 × 16.25cm)

6 6½-inch (16.25cm) long twigs

a piece of mirror measuring 6 × 8 inches
     (15 × 20cm)

2 12-inch (30cm) squares of red felt

a large rubber bat

a 24-inch (60cm) scarf or a 24-inch square
     piece of material

thumbtacks

white glue

Tack and glue pieces A, B and C together (1). Cover the back of piece D, the inside of the partially

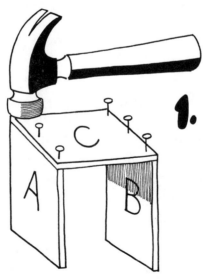

completed box and the back side of the mirror with red felt. Place a bead of white glue on the long edge of the mirror and insert in the box (2). Tack and glue piece D to complete the box (3).

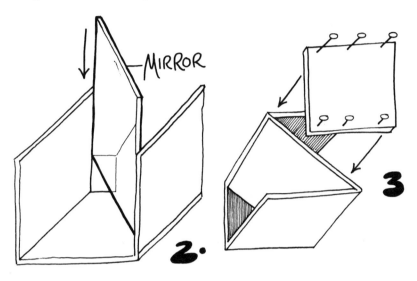

Place the rubber bat inside the red felt side of the box and secure with thumbtacks (4).

Glue the twigs to both openings so they look like cage bars.

After everything has set and dried, drape the scarf over the top of the box and secure it with thumbtacks (5).

The Thing in the Box

To make "The Thing in the Box," you'll need:
2 pieces of wood measuring 12 × 7 inches
    (30 × 17.5cm)
2 pieces of wood measuring 12 × 4 inches
    (30 × 10cm)
2 pieces of wood measuring 6½ × 3½ inches
    (16.25 × 8.75cm)
a square of black felt
a set of small hinges
black thread
a rubber monster-hand glove or a regular glove
cotton or shredded material for stuffing
thumbtacks
white glue

Using one of the larger pieces of wood as a base, make a box by gluing and nailing the other smaller pieces to it.

Cover the inside of the box with black felt material.

Use the remaining large piece of plywood as the lid, attaching it to the box at the 7-inch (17.5cm) wide end with the small hinges.

Stuff the glove with cotton or other stuffing filler.

Attach the upper end of the glove to the inside back of the box with thumbtacks (1).

Fasten the black thread to a thumbtack in the lid of the box, and tie it to the middle finger of the glove (2) so that when the lid is lifted, the glove is lifted out of the box as well.

Note: Although many joke and magic shops, particularly around Halloween, sell fake rubber hands, it's better to make your own stuffed glove hand. Fake rubber hands are harder to attach to the back of the box and, due to their increased weight, might break the thread attached to the lid.

The Creature Bag

For this basic "Creature Bag," you'll need:
a piece of material measuring 8 × 24 inches
     (20 × 60cm)
needle
thread

Fold about six inches (15cm) of the material to form the secret pocket and sew along the edges (1).

Fold the material in half with the pocket on the outside, and sew along both edges (2).

Turn the bag inside out, and you're ready to perform.

Note: For a more professional-looking bag, use a piece of 8 × 24-inch (20 × 60cm) black material and a piece of 8 × 18-inch (20 × 45cm) material in a color or pattern.

Sew the secret pocket into the piece of black material. Turn the black cloth over and sew the colored piece to the back. Fold in half with the colored material inside and sew both edges. Turn inside out.

Now you have a colorful bag with a black inside liner!

The Haunted House

For this prop, you'll need:

4 pieces of quarter-inch (4mm) plywood measuring
  5 × 7 inches (12.5 × 17.5cm)
a 46-ounce juice can
  (1.38 l juice tin)
a 24-ounce juice can (.7 l juice tin)
a piece of black cloth material
red construction paper
flat black paint
transparent tape
white glue
popsicle sticks

On one of the pieces of plywood, cut a center door one inch from the bottom, 3 inches (7.5cm) wide and 4 inches (10cm) high (1). Glue and tack the pieces together to form a box (2).

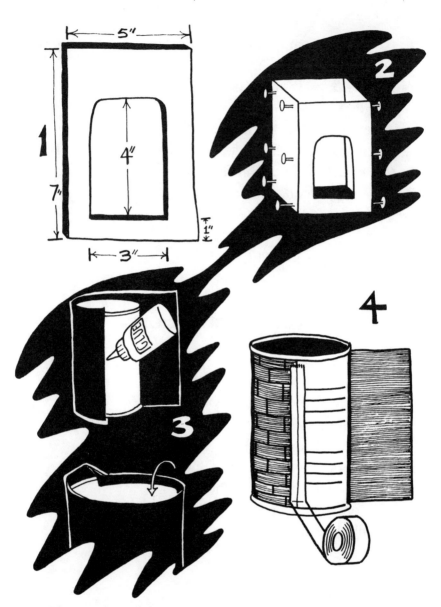

Thoroughly wash both tin cans and remove the labels. Remove both ends of the larger can.

Paint the inside of the box, tube and canister with flat black paint.

Glue the material (3) to the outside of the canister, making sure you cover it completely. Tuck the excess material inside the can and glue it down. This covers the rough edges caused by removing the lid so that the material you pull out during the performance won't snag.

Draw a brick design on the construction paper. Trim it so that it fits the outside of the tube (4). Secure it with tape, and wrap it around the tube so that it fits tightly. Close with additional tape.

Paint the outside of the box so that it looks like the exterior of an old, haunted house.

Note: To make the shingles at the top of the house shown in the illustration, glue two layers of ice cream sticks to the upper edge of the box before painting it.

Decorating Your Props

There are several schools of thought on how magical apparatus should look. Some magicians like their equipment painted and decorated in bright, circus colors. Some decorate it with oriental designs. Others like to give everything a dark and sinister look. Still others make everything look as ordinary and normal as possible.

Which is the best?

There is no set rule. Decorate your equipment to suit your own taste and tell your own story.

For example, you can make the face of the floating ghost scary, silly or even stupid. It all depends on the effect you want it to have on your audience.

You can paint "The Haunted House" to look like a creepy old house or a miniature haunted castle.

You could paint "The Vanishing Ghost Box" grey and paint the letters "R.I.P." on the right-hand door so it looks like a miniature tombstone!

Around Halloween many fabric stores sell material in very spooky patterns. Use some of this for an even scarier-looking "Creature Bag."

The Thing's box (page 86) looks good in glossy black paint, but painting it to look like a small packing crate covered with messages such as "Danger!," "Do Not Open," and "You'll Be Sorry" looks great and comical as well.

It's all up to you.

Let your imagination be your guide!

8. More Sinister Spells with Spooky Props

Now that you've built some Spooky Props, don't stop with the tricks explained in the previous chapters. There are lots of other things you can do with them.

Some Other Uses for
The Phantom Tube

"The Phantom Tube" can be used to change any small item into anything else that has already been loaded into the lower chamber.

Here are a couple of other ideas:

Place a red rubber ball about the same size as the Killer Tomato in the lower chamber of the phantom can.

After producing the Killer Tomato from the tomato tins, put it into the Phantom Tube. Once the Phantom Tube is turned over, spill out the ball and let it bounce into the audience.

Everyone will think the Killer Tomato is attacking!

You could also change the Killer Tomato into a bunch of fake sliced tomatoes for a comic effect, or into a red handkerchief to use in another trick.

Completely Batty

Here's a really great trick using "The Phantom Tube" that you can use in conjunction with "Bats in the Belfry" and "The Bat's Cage."

Fill the lower chamber of the Phantom Tube with a number of small rubber bats. After showing "The Bat's Cage," tell your audience you know where you can find the rest of the bats you expected to see.

Put a black handkerchief into the can.

Turn it over, take off the lid and toss the bats into the audience!

116

More Things to Do with
The Thing in the Box

In Chapter 6, "The Thing in the Box" is used to produce a key. Instead, you could tape a playing card to
the palm of the Thing. Make it a duplicate card of
the one you force in "The Card Prediction."

Instead of your predicting what the chosen card is,
tell your audience that your assistant, the Thing, will
find it for you.

Lift the lid, and there it is.

Here's something else you can do with The Thing.

Take a handkerchief identical to the one you use in
"A Spooky Knot," except put in it the wire gimmick

needed for "The Spirited Handkerchief." Place this hanky in the Thing Box so the knot is held between its fingers.

Do "A Spooky Knot," then make the handkerchief disappear using "The Vanishing Ghost Box."

Where did it go?

Lift the lid on "The Thing in the Box."

There it is!

Take it out and do "The Spirited Handkerchief."

As you can see, if you use "The Thing in the Box" in original and creative ways, it can be a quite "handy" assistant.

More Stuff from Inside
The Creature Bag

Another way to use "The Creature Bag" is to make an egg appear and disappear in the same way the spider and rat do.

Using a fake egg, you can do "The Creature Bag" as a follow-up trick to "The Ghostly Omelet" trick.

Here's how you do it. Select two volunteers to help you. Have one of them reach into the bag. No egg. Turn to the second and have him reach inside. Now there is an egg. Put it back in the bag and turn back to the first person. No egg. Twist the bag. Step on it. Nothing happens.

Now do "The Ghostly Omelet" trick.

After all the eggs you produce suddenly disappear, pick up the bag and have someone reach inside.

There, at last, is one of the eggs!

For a really startling effect, put a real egg in the bag.

When you take it out of the bag for the last time, crack it into a glass to prove it's real.

If you use a real egg, though, be careful!

You could easily wind up with egg on your face, to say nothing of inside your bag!

Opening Other Rooms in
The Haunted House

"The Haunted House" is not only a great production illusion, but it's actually a utility prop you can use as a setup for other tricks.

Almost everything used in the other magic tricks can be produced from the Haunted House.

Examples of how this works are detailed in the next chapter, "The Spookshow."

9. The Spookshow

Now that you've learned the tricks, it's time to put on a spookshow. To do this, you need to develop what's known as a routine.

Each trick you've learned is like a short story. A routine is more like a whole book in which each trick is a chapter. It's a combination of several tricks linked by logical transitions. This means that one trick leads naturally into the next by having something in common.

For example, turn to "1. Did Somebody See a Ghost?," where each trick tells a short story about a ghost. But if you perform "A Spooky Knot" followed by "The Phantom Tube," "The Floating Ghost" and "The Vanishing Ghost Box," you can tell a much more detailed story about the same ghost.

You can expand this story even further by adding "The Wand Through the Hanky" and "The Penetrating Key" to the routine. They will fit perfectly since the handkerchief used in "A Spooky Knot" is the same handkerchief used for these other tricks. Since it is the same one, it will really seem to have magical qualities that become even more magical when it's turned into "The Floating Ghost."

For a full routine, you could begin with "Bats in the Belfry," followed by "The Bat's Cage" and "The Haunted House." Make sure that the last item you produce from "The Haunted House" is the knotted handkerchief used for "A Spooky Knot" and then proceed with other tricks in Chapter 1, concluding with "The Vanishing Ghost Box."

If you performed this sequence of tricks, you would have told a full story that goes something like this:

There are bats around, but they're difficult to keep count of ("Bats in the Belfry"). You've only really seen one, but it isn't always there ("The Bat's Cage"). You know where the rest of them are—they're in a small haunted house ("The Haunted House"). There's also a ghost inside, one that likes to tie spooky knots in things ("A Spooky Knot") and create invisible holes ("Wand Through the Hanky" and "The Penetrating Key"). Even though he likes to pretend he's a hand-kerchief, he's only hiding. He really is a ghost ("The Phantom Tube") who floats around on his own ("The Floating Ghost"). But when all is said and done, he is just an illusion, because he was never really there ("The Vanishing Ghost Box").

You now have a routine.

As you read over the tricks in this book, you'll discover many ways to work them into additional routines. It's always good to think up two or three different routines to use, especially if you're showing your tricks to the same friends.

But never show the same trick over and over to the same people. The first time they see it, they'll be surprised. The second time they see it, however, they'll likely figure it out.

And magic is only truly wonderful when the methods remain secret.

So, like Dr. Frankenstein: Experiment.

Meanwhile, here are a couple of other routines you might try:

The Key to the Haunted House

1. Begin with all three parts of "The Thing in the Box."

2. Wave the key over "The Haunted House."

3. Produce the "Find the Ghost" picture cards from "The Haunted House."

4. Since the picture ghost isn't there, have him write a message. Do both parts of "The Ghost Writer."

5. Use the pencil to do "The Ghostly Touch."

6. Once again using the pencil, do "The Wand Through the Hanky."

7. Follow with "The Penetrating Key."

8. Use the key to perform "Through the Table."

9. Take out a second tumbler, and do "Tumbler Through Tumbler."

10. Finish by making the key disappear by doing "Key Through the Tumbler."

Time for the Spirits

1. Begin by producing the counting clock from "The Thing in the Box."

2. Find out when the ghosts will be around by doing "The Tell-Tale Timepiece."

3. Reach into the Thing's box and take out a deck of cards.

4. Do "The Floating Cards."

5. Follow it with either version of "The Rising Cards."

6. Then do either "The Card Prediction" or "Mind Reading II."

7. Leaving the cards in front of you, do "The Vanishing and Re-Appearing Wand."

8. Leaving the wand beside the cards, do "The Killer Tomato."

9. Placing the cans, killer tomato, wand and deck of cards on top of the counting clock, finish with "The Noisy Poltergeist."

Full of Holes

1. Begin with "Full of Holes."

2. Follow with "The Vanishing and Re-Appearing Wand."

3. Use the wand to do "The Wand Through the Hanky."

4. Use the handkerchief for "The Penetrating Key."

5. Use the key again for all three parts of "The Thing in the Box."

6. Take out "The Haunted House."

7. Take all the items produced from it, including the small bell, and finish the routine with "The Noisy Poltergeist."

Now it's your turn. See how many different routines you can come up with.

See how many stories you can make up to go along with the routines you create.

Most of all, have fun!

About the Author

David Knoles is an entertainment feature writer for Copley Los Angeles Newspapers and the former drama, film and entertainment critic for *The Palos Verdes Peninsula News* in Palos Verdes, California. A former member of the Society of American Magicians, he performed magic and illusion shows at schools, universities and theatre festivals throughout the Southern California area and, during the mid-1970s, operated "Madhatter's Magic School" for young performers. He currently resides in Redondo Beach, California, where he is hard at work on a second book of magic.

Index